The Tresp

Volume 3

Gilbert Parker

Alpha Editions

This edition published in 2024

ISBN : 9789362094483

Design and Setting By
Alpha Editions
www.alphaedis.com
Email - info@alphaedis.com

Contents

VOLUME 3.

CHAPTER XII

HE STANDS BETWEEN TWO WORLDS

The next morning he went down to the family solicitor's office. He had done so, off and on, for weeks. He spent the time in looking through old family papers, fishing out ancient documents, partly out of curiosity, partly from an unaccountable presentiment. He had been there about an hour this morning when a clerk brought him a small box, which, he said, had been found inside another box belonging to the Belward-Staplings, a distant branch of the family. These had asked for certain ancient papers lately, and a search had been made, with this result. The little box was not locked, and the key was in it. How the accident occurred was not difficult to imagine. Generations ago there had probably been a conference of the two branches of the family, and the clerk had inadvertently locked the one box within the other. This particular box of the Belward-Staplings was not needed again. Gaston felt that here was something. These hours spent among old papers had given him strange sensations, had, on the one hand, shown him his heritage; but had also filled him with the spirit of that by-gone time. He had grown further away from the present. He had played his part as in a drama: his real life was in the distant past and out in the land of the heathen.

Now he took out a bundle of papers with broken seals, and wound with a faded tape. He turned the rich important parchments over in his hands. He saw his own name on the outside of one: "Sir Gaston Robert Belward." And there was added: "Bart." He laughed. Well, why not complete the reproduction? He was an M. P.—why not a, Baronet? He knew how it was done. There were a hundred ways. Throw himself into the arbitration question between Canada and the United States: spend ten thousand pounds of—his grandfather's—money on the Party? His reply to himself was cynical: the game was not worth the candle. What had he got out of it all? Money? Yes: and he enjoyed that—the power that it gave— thoroughly. The rest? He knew that it did not strike as deep as it ought: the family tradition, the social scheme—the girl.

"What a brute I am!" he said. "I'm never wholly of it. I either want to do as they did when George Villiers had his innings, or play the gipsy as I did so many years."

The gipsy! As he held the papers in his hand he thought as he had done last night, of the gipsy-van on Ridley Common, and of—how well he remembered her name!—of Andree.

He suddenly threw his head back, and laughed. "Well, well, but it is droll! Last night, an English gentleman, an honourable member with the Treasury

Bench in view; this morning an adventurer, a Romany. I itch for change. And why? Why? I have it all, yet I could pitch it away this moment for a wild night on the slope, or a nigger hunt on the Rivas. Chateau-Leoville, Goulet, and Havanas at a bob?—Jove, I thirst for a swig of raw Bourbon and the bite of a penny Mexican! Games, Gaston, games! Why the devil did little Joe worry at being made 'move on'? I've got 'move on' in every pore: I'm the Wandering Jew. Oh, a gentleman born am I! But the Romany sweats from every inch of you, Gaston Belward! What was it that sailor on the Cyprian said of the other? 'For every hair of him was rope-yarn, and every drop of blood Stockholm tar!'"

He opened a paper. Immediately he was interested. Another; then, quickly, two more; and at last, getting to his feet with an exclamation, he held a document to the light, and read it through carefully. He was alone in the room. He calmly folded it up, put it in his pocket, placed the rest of the papers back, locked the box, and passing into the next room, gave it to the clerk. Then he went out, a curious smile on his face. He stopped presently on the pavement.

"But it wouldn't hold good, I fancy, after all these years. Yet Law is a queer business. Anyhow, I've got it."

An hour later he called on Mrs. Gasgoyne and Delia. Mrs. Gasgoyne was not at home. After a little while, Gaston, having listened to some extracts from the newspapers upon his "brilliant, powerful, caustic speech, infinite in promise of an important career," quietly told her that he was starting for Paris, and asked when they expected to go abroad in their yacht. Delia turned pale, and could not answer for a moment. Then she became very still, and as quietly answered that they expected to get away by the middle of August. He would join them? Yes, certainly, at Marseilles, or perhaps, Gibraltar. Her manner, so well-controlled, though her features seemed to shrink all at once, if it did not deceive him, gave him the wish to say an affectionate thing. He took her hand and said it. She thanked him, then suddenly dropped her fingers on his shoulder, and murmured with infinite gentleness and pride:

"You will miss me; you ought to!"

He drew the hand down.

"I could not forget you, Delia," he said.

Her eyes came up quickly, and she looked steadily, wonderingly at him.

"Was it necessary to say that?"

She was hurt—inexpressibly,—and she shrank. He saw that she misunderstood him; but he also saw that, on the face of it, the phrase was not complimentary. His reply was deeply kind, effective. There was a pause—

and the great moment for them both passed. Something ought to have happened. It did not. If she had had that touch of abandon shown when she sang "The Waking of the Fire," Gaston might, even at this moment, have broken his promise to his uncle; but, somehow, he knew himself slipping away from her. With the tenderness he felt, he still knew that he was acting; imitating, reproducing other, better, moments with her. He felt the disrespect to her, but it could not be helped—it could not be helped.

He said that he would call and say good-bye to her and Mrs. Gasgoyne at four o'clock. Then he left. He went to his chambers, gave Jacques instructions, did some writing, and returned at four. Mrs. Gasgoyne had not come back. She had telegraphed that she would not be in for lunch. There was nothing remarkable in Gaston's and Delia's farewell. She thought he looked worn, and ought to have change, showing in every word that she trusted him, and was anxious that he should be, as she put it gaily, "comfy." She was composed. The cleverest men are blind in the matter of a woman's affections; and Gaston was only a mere man, after all. He thought that she had gone about as far in the way of feeling as she could go.

Nevertheless, in his hansom, he frowned, and said: "I oughtn't to go. But I'm choking here. I can't play the game an hour longer without a change. I'll come back all right. I'll meet her in the Mediterranean after my kick-up, and it'll be all O. K. Jacques and I will ride down through Spain to Gibraltar, and meet the Kismet there. I shall have got rid of this restlessness then, and I'll be glad enough to settle down, pose for throne and constitution, cultivate the olive branch, and have family prayers."

At eight o'clock he appeared at Ridley Court, and bade his grandfather and grandmother good-bye. They were full of pride, and showed their affection in indirect ways—Sir William most by offering his opinion on the Bill and quoting Gaston frequently; Lady Belward, by saying that next year she would certainly go up to town—she had not done so for five years! They both agreed that a scamper on the Continent would now be good for him. At nine o'clock he passed the rectory, on his way, strange to note, to the church. There was one light burning, but it was not in the study nor in Alice's window. He supposed they had not returned. He paused and thought. If anything happened, she should know. But what should happen? He shook his head. He moved on to the church. The doors were unlocked. He went in, drew out a little pocket-lantern, lit it, and walked up the aisle.

"A sentimental business this: I don't know why I do it," he thought.

He stopped at the tomb of Sir Gaston Belward, put his hand on it, and stood looking at it.

"I wonder if there is anything in it?" he said aloud: "if he does influence me? if we've got anything to do with each other? What he did I seem to know somehow, more or less. A little dwarf up in my brain drops the nuts down now and then. Well, Sir Gaston Belward, what is going to be the end of all this? If we can reach across the centuries, why, good-night and goodbye to you. Good-bye."

He turned and went down the aisle. At the door a voice, a whispering voice, floated to him: "Good-bye."

He stopped short and listened. All was still. He walked up the aisle, and listened again.-Nothing! He stood before the tomb, looking at it curiously. He was pale, but collected. He raised the light above his head, and looked towards the altar.—Nothing! Then he went to the door again, and paused.—Nothing!

Outside he said

"I'd stake my life I heard it!"

A few minutes afterwards, a girl rose up from behind the organ in the chancel, and felt her way outside. It was Alice Wingfield, who had gone to the church to pray. It was her good-bye which had floated down to Gaston.

CHAPTER XIII

HE JOURNEYS AFAR

Politicians gossiped. Where was the new member? His friends could not tell, further than that he had gone abroad. Lord Faramond did not know, but fetched out his lower lip knowingly.

"The fellow has instinct for the game," he said. Sketches, portraits were in the daily and weekly journals, and one hardy journalist even gave an interview—which had never occurred. But Gaston remained a picturesque nine-days' figure, and then Parliament rose for the year.

Meanwhile he was in Paris, and every morning early he could be seen with Jacques riding up the Champs Elysee and out to the Bois de Boulogne. Every afternoon at three he sat for "Monmouth" or the "King of Ys" with his horse in his uncle's garden.

Ian Belward might have lived in a fashionable part; he preferred the Latin Quarter, with incursions into the other at fancy. Gaston lived for three days in the Boulevard Haussman, and then took apartments, neither expensive nor fashionable, in a quiet street. He was surrounded by students and artists, a few great men and a host of small men: Collarossi's school here and Delacluse's there: models flitting in and out of the studios in his court-yard, who stared at him as he rode, and sought to gossip with Jacques—accomplished without great difficulty.

Jacques was transformed. A cheerful hue grew on his face. He had been an exile, he was now at home. His French tongue ran, now with words in the patois of Normandy, now of Brittany; and all with the accent of French Canada, an accent undisturbed by the changes and growths of France. He gossiped, but no word escaped him which threw any light on his master's history.

Soon, in the Latin Quarter, they were as notable as they had been at Ridley Court or in London. On the Champs Elysee side people stared at the two: chiefly because of Gaston's splendid mount and Jacques's strange broncho. But they felt that they were at home. Gaston's French was not perfect, but it was enough for his needs. He got a taste of that freedom which he had handed over to the dungeons of convention two years before. He breathed. Everything interested him so much that the life he had led in England seemed very distant.

He wrote to Delia, of course. His letters were brief, most interesting, not tenderly intimate, and not daily. From the first they puzzled her a little, and continued to do so; but because her mother said, "What an impossible man!"

she said, "Perfectly possible! Of course he is not like other men; he is a genius."

And the days went on.

Gaston little loved the purlieus of the Place de l'Opera. One evening at a club in the Boulevard Malesherbes bored him. It was merely Anglo- American enjoyment, dashed with French drama. The Bois was more to his taste, for he could stretch his horse's legs; but every day he could be found before some simple cafe in Montparnasse, sipping vermouth, and watching the gay, light life about him. He sat up with delight to see an artist and his "Madame" returning from a journey in the country, seated upon sheaves of corn, quite unregarded by the world; doing as they listed with unabashed simplicity. He dined often at the little Hotel St. Malo near the Gare Montparnasse, where the excellent landlord played the host, father, critic, patron, comrade—often benefactor—to his bons enfants. He drank vin ordinaire, smoked caporal cigarettes, made friends, and was in all as a savage—or a much-travelled English gentleman.

His uncle Ian had introduced him here as at other places of the kind, and, whatever his ulterior object was, had an artist's pleasure at seeing a layman enjoy the doings of Paris art life. Himself lived more luxuriously. In an avenue not far from the Luxembourg he had a small hotel with a fine old-fashioned garden behind it, and here distinguished artists, musicians, actors, and actresses came at times.

The evening of Gaston's arrival he took him to a cafe and dined him, and afterwards to the Boullier—there, merely that he might see; but this place had nothing more than a passing interest for him. His mind had the poetry of a free, simple—even wild-life, but he had no instinct for vice in the name of amusement. But the later hours spent in the garden under the stars, the cheerful hum of the boulevards coming to them distantly, stung his veins like good wine. They sat and talked, with no word of England in it at all, Jacques near, listening.

Ian Belward was at his best: genial, entertaining, with the art of the man of no principles, no convictions, and a keen sense of life's sublime incongruities. Even Jacques, whose sense of humour had grown by long association with Gaston, enjoyed the piquant conversation. The next evening the same. About ten o'clock a few men dropped in: a sculptor, artists, and Meyerbeer, an American newspaper correspondent—who, however, was not known as such to Gaston.

This evening Ian determined to make Gaston talk. To deepen a man's love for a thing, get him to talk of it to the eager listener—he passes from the narrator to the advocate unconsciously. Gaston was not to talk of England, but of the North, of Canada, of Mexico, the Lotos Isles. He did so picturesquely, yet simply too, in imperfect but sufficient French. But as he told of one striking incident in the Rockies, he heard Jacques make a quick expression of dissent. He smiled. He had made some mistake in detail. Now, Jacques had been in his young days in Quebec the village story-teller; one who, by inheritance or competency, becomes semi- officially a raconteur for the parish; filling in winter evenings, nourishing summer afternoons, with tales, weird, childlike, daring.

Now Gaston turned and said to Jacques:

"Well, Brillon, I've forgotten, as you see; tell them how it was."

Two hours later when Jacques retired on some errand, amid ripe applause, Ian said:

"You've got an artist there, Cadet: that description of the fight with the loop garoo was as good as a thing from Victor Hugo. Hugo must have heard just such yarns, and spun them on the pattern. Upon my soul, it's excellent stuff. You've lived, you two."

Another night Ian Belward gave a dinner, at which were present an actress, a singer of some repute, the American journalist, and others. Something that was said sent Gaston's mind to the House of Commons. Presently he saw himself in a ridiculous picture: a buffalo dragging the Treasury Bench about the Chamber; as one conjures things in an absurd dream. He laughed outright, at a moment when Mademoiselle Cerise was telling of a remarkable effect she produced one night in "Fedora," unpremeditated, inspired; and Mademoiselle Cerise, with smiling lips and eyes like daggers, called him a bear. This brought him to him self, and he swam with the enjoyment. He did enjoy it, but not as his uncle wished and hoped. Gaston did not respond eagerly to the charms of Mademoiselle Cerise and Madame Juliette.

Was Delia, then, so strong in the barbarian's mind? He could not think so, but Gaston had not shown yet, either for model, for daughter of joy, or for the mademoiselles of the stage any disposition to an amour or a misalliance; and either would be interesting and sufficient! Models went in and out of Ian's studio and the studios of others, and Gaston chatted with them at times; and once he felt the bare arm and bare breast of a girl as she sat for a nymph, and said in an interested way that her flesh was as firm and fine as a Tongan's. He even disputed with his uncle on the tints of her skin, on seeing him paint it in, showing a fine eye for colour. But there was nothing more; he was impressed, observant, interested—that was all. His uncle began to wonder if the Englishman was, after all, deeper in the grain than the savage. He contented himself with the belief that the most vigorous natures are the most difficult to rouse. Mademoiselle Cerise sang, with chic and abandon very fascinating to his own sensuous nature, a song with a charming air and sentiment. It was after a night at the opera when they had seen her in "Lucia," and the contrast, as she sang in his garden, softly lighted, showed her at the most attractive angles. She drifted from a sparkling chanson to the delicate pathos of a song of De Musset's.

Gaston responded to the artist; but to the woman—no. He had seen a new life, even in its abandon, polite, fresh. It amused him, but he could still turn to the remembrance of Delia without blushing, for he had come to this in the spirit of the idler, not the libertine. Mademoiselle Cerise said to Ian at last:

"Enfin, is the man stone? As handsome as a leopard, too! But, it is no matter."

She made another effort to interest him, however. It galled her that he did not fall at her feet as others had done. Even Ian had come there in his day, but she knew him too well. She had said to him at the time: "You, monsieur? No, thank you. A week, a month, and then the brute in you would out. You make a woman fond, and then—a mat for your feet, and your wicked smile, and savage English words to drive her to the vitriol or the Seine. Et puis, dear monsieur, accept my good friendship; nothing more. I will sing to you, dance to you, even pray for you—we poor sinners do that sometimes, and go on sinning; but, again, nothing more."

Ian admired her all the more for her refusal of him, and they had been good friends. He had told her of his nephew's coming, had hinted at his fortune, at his primitive soul, at the unconventional strain in him, even at marriage. She could not read his purpose, but she knew there was something, and answering him with a yes, had waited. Had Gaston have come to her feet she would probably have got at the truth somehow, and have worked in his favour—the joy vice takes to side with virtue, at times—when it is at no personal sacrifice. But Gaston was superior in a grand way. He was simple, courteous, interested only. This stung her, and she would bring him to his knees, if she could. This night she had rung all the changes, and had done no more than get his frank applause. She became petulant in an airy, exacting way. She asked him about his horse. This interested him. She wanted to see it. To-morrow? No, no, now. Perhaps to-morrow she would not care to; there was no joy in deliberate pleasure. Now—now—now! He laughed. Well then, now, as she wished!

Jacques was called. She said to him:

"Come here, little comrade." Jacques came. "Look at me," she added. She fixed her eyes on him, and smiled. She was in the soft flare of the lights.

"Well," she said after a moment, "what do you think of me?"

Jacques was confused. "Madame is beautiful."

"The eyes?" she urged.

"I have been to Gaspe, and west to Esquimault, and in England, but I have never seen such as those," he said. Race and primitive man spoke there.

She laughed. "Come closer, little man."

He did so. She suddenly rose, dropped her hands on his shoulders, and kissed his cheek.

"Now bring the horse, and I will kiss him too."

Did she think she could rouse Gaston by kissing his servant? Yet it did not disgust him. He knew it was a bit of acting, and it was well done. Besides, Jacques Brillon was not a mere servant, and he, too, had done well. She sat back and laughed lightly when Jacques was gone. Then she said: "The honest fellow!" and hummed an air:

"'The pretty coquette
Well she needs to be wise,
Though she strike to the heart
By a glance of her eyes.

"'For the daintiest bird
Is the sport of the storm,
And the rose fadeth most
When the bosom is warm.'"

In twenty minutes the gate of the garden opened, and Jacques appeared with Saracen. The horse's black skin glistened in the lights, and he tossed his head and champed his bit. Gaston rose. Mademoiselle Cerise sprang to her feet and ran forward. Jacques put out his hand to stop her, and Gaston caught her shoulder. "He's wicked with strangers," Gaston said. "Chat!" she rejoined, stepped quickly to the horse's head and, laughing, put out her hand to stroke him. Jacques caught the beast's nose, and stopped a lunge of the great white teeth.

"Enough, madame, he will kill you!"

"Yet I am beautiful—is it not so?"

"The poor beast is ver' blind."

"A pretty compliment," she rejoined, yet angry at the beast.

Gaston came, took the animal's head in his hands, and whispered. Saracen became tranquil. Gaston beckoned to Mademoiselle Cerise. She came. He took her hand in his and put it at the horse's lips. The horse whinnied angrily at first, but permitted a caress from the actress's fingers.

"He does not make friends easily," said Gaston. "Nor does his master."

Her eyes lifted to his, the lids drooping suggestively. "But when the pact is made—!"

"Till death us do part?"

"Death or ruin."

"Death is better."

"That depends!"

"Ah! I understand," she said.

"On—the woman?"

"Yes."

Then he became silent. "Mount the horse," she urged.

Gaston sprang at one bound upon the horse's bare back. Saracen reared and wheeled.

"Splendid!" she said; then, presently: "Take me up with you."

He looked doubting for a moment, then whispered to the horse.

"Come quickly," he said.

She came to the side of the horse. He stooped, caught her by the waist, and lifted her up. Saracen reared, but Gaston had him down in a moment.

Ian Belward suddenly called out:

"For God's sake, keep that pose for five minutes—only five!" He caught up some canvas. "Hold candles near them," he said to the others. They did so. With great swiftness he sketched in the strange picture. It looked weird, almost savage: Gaston's large form, his legs loose at the horse's side, the woman in her white drapery clinging to him.

In a little time the artist said:

"There; that will do. Ten such sittings and my 'King of Ys' will have its day with the world. I'd give two fortunes for the chance of it."

The woman's heart had beat fast with Gaston's arm around her. He felt the thrill of the situation. Man, woman, and horse were as of a piece.

But Cerise knew, when Gaston let her to the ground again, that she had not conquered.

CHAPTER XIV

IN WHICH THE PAST IS REPEATED

Next morning Gaston was visited by Meyerbeer the American journalist, of whose profession he was still ignorant. He saw him only as a man of raw vigour of opinion, crude manners, and heavy temperament. He had not been friendly to him at night, and he was surprised at the morning visit. The hour was such that Gaston must ask him to breakfast. The two were soon at the table of the Hotel St. Malo. Meyerbeer sniffed the air when he saw the place. The linen was ordinary, the rooms small; but all—he did not take this into account—irreproachably clean. The walls were covered with pictures; some taken for unpaid debts, gifts from students since risen to fame or gone into the outer darkness,—to young artists' eyes, the sordid moneymaking world,—and had there been lost; from a great artist or two who remembered the days of his youth and the good host who had seen many little colonies of artists come and go.

They sat down to the table, which was soon filled with students and artists. Then Meyerbeer began to see, not only an interesting thing, but "copy." He was, in fact, preparing a certain article which, as he said to himself, would "make 'em sit up" in London and New York. He had found out Gaston's history, had read his speech in the Commons, had seen paragraphs speculating as to where he was; and now he, Salem Meyerbeer, would tell them what the wild fellow was doing. The Bullier, the cafes in the Latin Quarter, apartments in a humble street, dining for one- franc-fifty, supping with actresses, posing for the King of Ys with that actress in his arms—all excellent in their way. But now there was needed an entanglement, intrigue, amour, and then America should shriek at his picture of one of the British aristocracy, and a gentleman of the Commons, "on the loose," as he put it.

He would head it:

"ARISTOCRAT, POLITICIAN, LIBERTINE!"

Then, under that he would put:

> "CAN THE ETHIOPIAN CHANGE HIS SKIN, OR THE LEOPARD HIS SPOTS?" Jer. xi. 23.

The morality of such a thing? Morality only had to do with ruining a girl's name, or robbery. How did it concern this?

So Mr. Meyerbeer kept his ears open. Presently one of the students said to Bagshot, a young artist: "How does the dompteuse come on?"

"Well, I think it's chic enough. She's magnificent. The colour of her skin against the lions was splendid to-day: a regular rich gold with a sweet stain of red like a leaf of maize in September. There's never been such a Una. I've got my chance; and if I don't pull it off,

> 'Wrap me up in my tarpaulin jacket,
> And say a poor buffer lies low!'"

"Get the jacket ready," put in a young Frenchman, sneering.

The Englishman's jaw hardened, but he replied coolly

"What do you know about it?"

"I know enough. The Comte Ploare visits her."

"How the devil does that concern my painting her?" There was iron in Bagshot's voice.

"Who says you are painting her?"

The insult was conspicuous. Gaston quickly interposed. His clear strong voice rang down the table: "Will you let me come and see your canvas some day soon, Mr. Bagshot? I remember your picture 'A Passion in the Desert,' at the Academy this year. A fine thing: the leopard was free and strong. As an Englishman, I am proud to meet you."

The young Frenchman stared. The quarrel had passed to a new and unexpected quarter. Gaston's large, solid body, strong face, and penetrating eyes were not to be sneered out of sight. The Frenchman, an envious, disappointed artist, had had in his mind a bloodless duel, to give a fillip to an unacquired fame. He had, however, been drinking. He flung an insolent glance to meet Gaston's steady look, and said:

"The cock crows of his dunghill!"

Gaston looked at the landlord, then got up calmly and walked down the table. The Frenchman, expecting he knew not what, sprang to his feet, snatching up a knife; but Gaston was on him like a hawk, pinioning his arms and lifting him off the ground, binding his legs too, all so tight that the Frenchman squealed for breath.

"Monsieur," said Gaston to the landlord, "from the door or the window?"

The landlord was pale. It was in some respects a quarrel of races. For, French and English at the tables had got up and were eyeing each other. As to the immediate outcome of the quarrel, there could be no doubt. The English and Americans could break the others to pieces; but neither wished that. The landlord decided the matter:

"Drop him from this window."

He pushed a shutter back, and Gaston dropped the fellow on the hard pavement—a matter of five feet. The Frenchman got up raging, and made for the door; but this time he was met by the landlord, who gave him his hat, and bade him come no more. There was applause from both English and French. The journalist chuckled—another column!

Gaston had acted with coolness and common-sense; and when he sat down and began talking of the Englishman's picture again as if nothing had happened, the others followed, and the meal went on cheerfully.

Presently another young English painter entered, and listened to the conversation, which Gaston brought back to Una and the lions. It was his way to force things to his liking, if possible; and he wanted to hear about the woman—why, he did not ask himself. The new arrival, Fancourt by name, kept looking at him quizzically. Gaston presently said that he would visit the menagerie and see this famous dompteuse that afternoon.

"She's a brick," said Bagshot. "I was in debt, a year behind with my Pelletier here, and it took all I got for 'A Passion in the Desert' to square up. I'd nothing to go on with. I spent my last sou in visiting the menagerie. There I got an idea. I went to her, told her how I was fixed, and begged her to give me a chance. By Jingo! she brought the water to my eyes. Some think she's a bit of a devil; but she can be a devil of a saint, that's all I've got to say."

"Zoug-Zoug's responsible for the devil," said Fancourt to Bagshot.

"Shut up, Fan," rejoined Bagshot, hurriedly, and then whispered to him quickly.

Fancourt sent self-conscious glances down the table towards Gaston; and then a young American, newly come to Paris, said:

"Who's Zoug-Zoug, and what's Zoug-Zoug?"

"It's milk for babes, youngster," answered Bagshot quickly, and changed the conversation.

Gaston saw something strange in the little incident; but he presently forgot it for many a day, and then remembered it for many a day, when the wheel had spun through a wild arc.

When they rose from the table, Meyerbeer went to Bagshot, and said:

"Say, who's Zoug-Zoug, anyway?" Bagshot coolly replied:

"I'm acting for another paper. What price?"

"Fifty dollars," in a low voice, eagerly. Bagshot meditated.

"H'm, fifty dollars! Two hundred and fifty francs, or thereabouts. Beggarly!"

"A hundred, then."

Bagshot got to his feet, lighting a cigarette.

"Want to have a pretty story against a woman, and to smutch a man, do you? Well, I'm hard up; I don't mind gossip among ourselves; but sell the stuff to you—I'll see you damned first!"

This was said sufficiently loud; and after that, Meyerbeer could not ask Fancourt, so he departed with Gaston, who courteously dismissed him, to his astonishment and regret, for he had determined to visit the menagerie with his quarry.

Gaston went to his apartments, and cheerily summoned Jacques.

"Now, little man, for a holiday! The menagerie: lions, leopards, and a grand dompteuse; and afterwards dinner with me at the Cafe Blanche. I want a blow-out of lions and that sort. I'd like to be a lion-tamer myself for a month, or as long as might be."

He caught Jacques by the shoulders—he had not done so since that memorable day at Ridley Court. "See, Jacques, we'll do this every year. Six months in England, and three months on the Continent,—in your France, if you like,—and three months in the out-of-the-wayest place, where there'll be big game. Hidalgos for six months, Goths for the rest."

A half-hour later they were in the menagerie. They sat near the doors where the performers entered. For a long time they watched the performance with delight, clapping and calling bravo like boys. Presently the famous dompteuse entered,—Mademoiselle Victorine,—passing just below Gaston. He looked down, interested, at the supple, lithe creature making for the cages of lions in the amphitheatre. The figure struck him as familiar. Presently the girl turned, throwing a glance round the theatre. He caught the dash of the dark, piercing eyes, the luminous look, the face unpainted—in its own natural colour: neither hot health nor paleness, but a thing to bear the light of day. "Andree the gipsy!" he exclaimed in a low tone.

In less than two years this! Here was fame. A wanderer, an Ishmael then, her handful of household goods and her father in the grasp of the Law: to-day, Mademoiselle Victorine, queen of animal-tamers! And her name associated with the Comte Ploare!

With the Comte Ploare? Had it come to that? He remembered the look in her face when he bade her good-bye. Impossible! Then, immediately he laughed.

Why impossible? And why should he bother his head about it? People of this sort: Mademoiselle Cerise, Madame Juliette, Mademoiselle Victorine— what were they to him, or to themselves?

There flashed through his brain three pictures: when he stood by the bedside of the old dying Esquimaux in Labrador, and took a girl's hand in his; when among the flowers at Peppingham he heard Delia say: "Oh, Gaston! Gaston!" and Alice's face at midnight in the moonlit window at Ridley Court.

How strange this figure—spangled, gaudy, standing among her lions—seemed by these. To think of her, his veins thumping thus, was an insult to all three: to Delia, one unpardonable. And yet he could not take his eyes off her. Her performance was splendid. He was interested, speculative. She certainly had flown high; for, again, why should not a dompteuse be a decent woman? And here were money, fame of a kind, and an occupation that sent his blood bounding. A dompteur! He had tamed moose, and young mountain lions, and a catamount, and had had mad hours with pumas and arctic bears; and he could understand how even he might easily pass from M.P. to dompteur. It was not intellectual, but it was power of a kind; and it was decent, and healthy, and infinitely better than playing the Jew in business, or keeping a tavern, or "shaving" notes, and all that. Truly, the woman was to be admired, for she was earning an honest living; and no doubt they lied when they named her with Count Ploare. He kept coming back to that—Count Ploare! Why could they not leave these women alone? Did they think none of them virtuous? He would stake his life that Andree—he would call her that—was as straight as the sun.

"What do you think of her, Jacques?" he said suddenly.

"It is grand. Mon Dieu, she is wonderful—and a face all fire!"

Presently she came out of the cage, followed by two great lions. She walked round the ring, a hand on the head of each: one growling, the other purring against her, with a ponderous kind of affection. She talked to them as they went, giving occasionally a deep purring sound like their own. Her talk never ceased. She looked at the audience, but only as in a dream. Her mind was all with the animals. There was something splendid in it: she, herself, was a noble animal; and she seemed entirely in place where she was. The lions were fond of her, and she of them; but the first part of her performance had shown that they could be capricious. A lion's love is but a lion's love after all—and hers likewise, no doubt! The three seemed as one in their beauty, the woman superbly superior. Meyerbeer, in a far corner, was still on the trail of his sensation. He thought that he might get an article out of it—with the help of Count Ploare and Zoug-Zoug. Who was Zoug-Zoug? He exulted in her picturesqueness, and he determined to lie in wait. He thought it a pity that Comte Ploare was not an Englishman or an American; but it couldn't be helped. Yes, she was, as he said to himself, "a stunner." Meanwhile he watched Gaston, noted his intense interest.

Presently the girl stopped beside the cage. A chariot was brought out, and the two lions were harnessed to it. Then she called out another larger lion, which came unwillingly at first. She spoke sharply, and then struck him. He growled, but came on. Then she spoke softly to him, and made that peculiar purr, soft and rich. Now he responded, walked round her, coming closer, till his body made a half-circle about her, and his head was at her knees. She dropped her hand on it. Great applause rang through the building. This play had been quite accidental. But there lay one secret of the girl's success. She was original; she depended greatly on the power of the moment for her best effects, and they came at unexpected times.

It was at this instant that, glancing round the theatre in acknowledgment of the applause, her eyes rested mechanically on Gaston's box. There was generally some one important in that box: from a foreign prince to a young gentleman whose proudest moment was to take off his hat in the Bois to the queen of a lawless court. She had tired of being introduced to princes. What could it mean to her? And for the young bloods, whose greatest regret was that they could not send forth a daughter of joy into the Champs Elysee in her carriage, she had ever sent them about their business. She had no corner of pardon for them. She kissed her lions, she hugged the lion's cub that rode back and forth with her to the menagerie day by day—her companion in her modest apartments; but sell one of these kisses to a young gentleman of Paris, whose ambition was to master all the vices, and then let the vices master him!—she had not come to that, though, as she said in some bitter moments, she had come far.

Count Ploare—there was nothing in that. A blase man of the world, who had found it all not worth the bothering about, neither code nor people— he saw in this rich impetuous nature a new range of emotions, a brief return to the time when he tasted an open strong life in Algiers, in Tahiti. And he would laugh at the world by marrying her—yes, actually marrying her, the dompteuse! Accident had let him render her a service, not unimportant, once at Versailles, and he had been so courteous and considerate afterwards, that she had let him see her occasionally, but never yet alone. He soon saw that an amour was impossible. At last he spoke of marriage. She shook her head. She ought to have been grateful, but she was not. Why should she be? She did not know why he wished to marry her; but, whatever the reason, he was selfish. Well, she would be selfish. She did not care for him. If she married him, it would be because she was selfish: because of position, ease; for protection in this shameless Paris; and for a home, she who had been a wanderer since her birth.

It was mere bargaining. But at last her free, independent nature revolted. No: she had had enough of the chain, and the loveless hand of man, for three months that were burned into her brain—no more! If ever she loved—all; but not the right for Count Ploare to demand the affection she gave her lions freely.

The manager of the menagerie had tried for her affections, had offered a price for her friendship; and failing, had become as good a friend as such a man could be. She even visited his wife occasionally, and gave gifts to his children; and the mother trusted her and told her her trials. And so the thing went on, and the people talked.

As we said, she turned her eyes to Gaston's box. Instantly they became riveted, and then a deep flush swept slowly up her face and burned into her splendid hair. Meyerbeer was watching through his opera-glasses. He gave an exclamation of delight:

"By the holy smoke, here's something!" he said aloud.

For an instant Gaston and the girl looked at each other intently. He made a slight sign of recognition with his hand, and then she turned away, gone a little pale now. She stood looking at her lions, as if trying to recollect herself. The lion at her feet helped her. He had a change of temper, and, possibly fretting under inaction, growled. At once she summoned him to get into the chariot. He hesitated, but did so. She put the reins in his paws and took her place behind. Then a robe of purple and ermine was thrown over her shoulders by an attendant; she gave a sharp command, and the lions came round the ring, to wild applause. Even a Parisian audience had never seen anything like this. It was amusing too; for the coachman-lion was evidently disgusted with his task, and growled in a helpless kind of way.

As they passed Gaston's box, they were very near. The girl threw one swift glance; but her face was well controlled now. She heard, however, a whispered word come to her:

"Andree!"

A few moments afterwards she retired, and the performance was in other and less remarkable hands. Presently the manager himself came, and said that Mademoiselle Victorine would be glad to see Monsieur Belward if he so wished. Gaston left Jacques, and went.

Meyerbeer noticed the move, and determined to see the meeting if possible. There was something in it, he was sure. He would invent an excuse, and make his way behind.

Gaston and the manager were in the latter's rooms waiting for Victorine. Presently a messenger came, saying that Monsieur Belward would find

Mademoiselle in her dressing-room. Thither Gaston went, accompanied by the manager, who, however, left him at the door, nodding good-naturedly to Victorine, and inwardly praying that here was no danger to his business, for Victorine was a source of great profit. Yet he had failed himself, and all others had failed in winning her—why should this man succeed, if that was his purpose?

There was present an elderly, dark-featured Frenchwoman, who was always with Victorine, vigilant, protective, loving her as her own daughter.

"Monsieur!" said Andree, a warm colour in her cheek. Gaston shook her hand cordially, and laughed. "Mademoiselle—Andree?"

He looked inquiringly. "Yes, to you," she said.

"You have it all your own way now—isn't it so?" "With the lions, yes. Please sit down. This is my dear keeper," she said, touching the woman's shoulder. Then, to the woman: "Annette, you have heard me speak of this gentleman?"

The woman nodded, and modestly touched Gaston's outstretched hand.

"Monsieur was kind once to my dear Mademoiselle," she said.

Gaston cheerily smiled:

"Nothing, nothing, upon my word!" Presently he continued:

"Your father, what of him?" She sighed and shivered a little.

"He died in Auvergne three months after you saw him."

"And you?" He waved a hand towards the menagerie.

"It is a long story," she answered, not meeting his eyes. "I hated the Romany life. I became an artist's model; sickened of that,"—her voice went quickly here, "joined a travelling menagerie, and became what I am. That in brief."

"You have done well," he said admiringly, his face glowing.

"I am a successful dompteuse," she replied.

She then asked him who was his companion in the box. He told her. She insisted on sending for Jacques. Meanwhile they talked of her profession, of the animals. She grew eloquent. Jacques arrived, and suddenly remembered Andree—stammered, was put at his ease, and dropped into talk with Annette. Gaston fell into reminiscences of wild game, and talked intelligently, acutely of her work. He must wait, she said, until the performance closed, and then she would show him the animals as a happy family. Thus a half-hour went by.

Meanwhile, Meyerbeer had asked the manager to take him to Mademoiselle; but was told that Victorine never gave information to journalists, and would not be interviewed. Besides, she had a visitor. Yes, Meyerbeer knew it—Mr. Gaston Belward; but that did not matter. The manager thought it did matter. Then, with an idea of the future, Meyerbeer asked to be shown the menagerie thoroughly—he would write it up for England and America.

And so it happened that there were two sets of people inspecting the menagerie after the performance. Andree let a dozen of the animals out—lions, leopards, a tiger, and a bear,—and they gambolled round her playfully, sometimes quarrelling with each other, but brought up smartly by her voice and a little whip, which she always carried—the only sign of professional life about her, though there was ever a dagger hid in her dress. For the rest, she looked a splendid gipsy.

Gaston suddenly asked if he might visit her. At the moment she was playing with the young tiger. She paused, was silent, preoccupied. The tiger, feeling neglected, caught her hand with its paw, tearing the skin. Gaston whipped out his handkerchief, and stanched the blood. She wrapped the handkerchief quickly round her hand, and then, recovering herself, ordered the animals back into their cages. They trotted away, and the attendant locked them up. Meanwhile Jacques had picked up and handed to Gaston a letter, dropped when he drew out his handkerchief. It was one received two days before from Delia Gasgoyne. He had a pang of confusion, and hastily put it into his pocket.

Up to this time there had been no confusion in his mind. He was going back to do his duty; to marry the girl, union with whom would be an honour; to take his place in his kingdom. He had had no minute's doubt of that. It was necessary, and it should be done. The girl? Did he not admire her, honour her, care for her? Why, then, this confusion?

Andree said to him that he might come the next morning for breakfast. She said it just as the manager and Meyerbeer passed her. Meyerbeer heard it, and saw the look in the faces of both: in hers, bewildered, warm, penetrating; in Gaston's, eager, glowing, bold, with a distant kind of trouble.

Here was a thickening plot for Paul Pry. He hugged himself. But who was Zoug-Zoug? If he could but get at that! He asked the manager, who said he did not know. He asked a dozen men that evening, but none knew. He would ask Ian Belward. What a fool not to have thought of him at first. He knew all the gossip of Paris, and was always communicative—but was he, after all? He remembered now that the painter had a way of talking at discretion: he had never got any really good material from him. But he would try him in this.

So, as Gaston and Jacques travelled down the Boulevard Montparnasse, Meyerbeer was not far behind. The journalist found Ian Belward at home, in a cynical indolent mood.

"Wherefore Meyerbeer?" he said, as he motioned the other to a chair, and pushed over vermouth and cigarettes.

"To ask a question."

"One question? Come, that's penance. Aren't you lying as usual?"

"No; one only. I've got the rest of it."

"Got the rest of it, eh? Nasty mess you've got, whatever it is, I'll be bound. What a nice mob you press fellows are—wholesale scavengers!"

"That's all right. This vermouth is good enough. Well, will you answer my question?"

"Possibly, if it's not personal. But Lord knows where your insolence may run! You may ask if I'll introduce you to a decent London club!"

Meyerbeer flushed at last.

"You're rubbing it in," he said angrily.

He did wish to be introduced to a good London club. "The question isn't personal, I guess. It's this: Who's Zoug-Zoug?"

Smoke had come trailing out of Belward's nose, his head thrown back, his eyes on the ceiling. It stopped, and came out of his mouth on one long, straight whiff. Then the painter brought his head to a natural position slowly, and looking with a furtive nonchalance at Meyerbeer, said:

"Who is what?"

"Who's Zoug-Zoug?"

"That is your one solitary question, is it?"

"That's it."

"Very well. Now, I'll be scavenger. What is the story? Who is the woman—for you've got a woman in it, that's certain?"

"Will you tell me, then, whether you know Zoug-Zoug?"

"Yes."

"The woman is Mademoiselle Victorine, the dompteuse."

"Ah, I've not seen her yet. She burst upon Paris while I was away. Now, straight: no lies: who are the others?"

Meyerbeer hesitated; for, of course, he did not wish to speak of Gaston at this stage in the game. But he said:

"Count Ploare—and Zoug-Zoug."

"Why don't you tell me the truth?"

"I do. Now, who is Zoug-Zoug?"

"Find out."

"You said you'd tell me."

"No. I said I'd tell you if I knew Zoug-Zoug. I do."

"That's all you'll tell me?"

"That's all. And see, scavenger, take my advice and let Zoug-Zoug alone. He's a man of influence; and he's possessed of a devil. He'll make you sorry, if you meddle with him!"

He rose, and Meyerbeer did the same, saying: "You'd better tell me."

"Now, don't bother me. Drink your vermouth, take that bundle of cigarettes, and hunt Zoug-Zoug else where. If you find him, let me know. Good-bye."

Meyerbeer went out furious. The treatment had been too heroic.

"I'll give a sweet savour to your family name," he said with an oath, as he shook his fist at the closed door. Ian Belward sat back and looked at the ceiling reflectively.

"H'm!" he said at last. "What the devil does this mean? Not Andree, surely not Andree! Yet I wasn't called Zoug-Zoug before that. It was Bagshot's insolent inspiration at Auvergne. Well, well!"

He got up, drew over a portfolio of sketches, took out two or three, put them in a row against a divan, sat down, and looked at them half quizzically.

"It was rough on you, Andree; but you were hard to please, and I am constant to but one. Yet, begad, you had solid virtues; and I wish, for your sake, I had been a different kind of fellow. Well, well, we'll meet again some time, and then we'll be good friends, no doubt."

He turned away from the sketches and picked up some illustrated newspapers. In one was a portrait. He looked at it, then at the sketches again and again.

"There's a resemblance," he said. "But no, it's not possible. Andree-Mademoiselle Victorine! That would be amusing. I'd go to-morrow and see, if I weren't off to Fontainebleau. But there's no hurry: when I come back will do."

CHAPTER XV

WHEREIN IS SEEN THE OLD ADAM AND THE GARDEN

At Ridley Court and Peppingham all was serene to the eye. Letters had come to the Court at least once every two weeks from Gaston, and the minds of the Baronet and his wife were at ease. They even went so far as to hope that he would influence his uncle; for it was clear to them both that whatever Gaston's faults were, they were agreeably different from Ian's. His fame and promise were sweet to their nostrils. Indeed, the young man had brought the wife and husband nearer than they had been since Robert vanished over-sea. Each had blamed the other in an indefinite, secret way; but here was Robert's son, on whom they could lavish—as they did—their affection, long since forfeited by Ian. Finally, one day, after a little burst of thanksgiving, on getting an excellent letter from Gaston, telling of his simple, amusing life in Paris, Sir William sent him one thousand pounds, begging him to buy a small yacht, or to do what he pleased with it.

"A very remarkable man, my dear," Sir William said, as he enclosed the cheque. "Excellent wisdom—excellent!"

"Who could have guessed that he knew so much about the poor and the East End, and all those social facts and figures?" Lady Belward answered complacently.

"An unusual mind, with a singular taste for history, and yet a deep observation of the present. I don't know when and how he does it. I really do not know."

"It is nice to think that Lord Faramond approves of him."

"Most noticeable. And we have not been a Parliamentary family since the first Charles's time. And then it was a Gaston. Singular—quite singular! Coincidences of looks and character. Nature plays strange games. Reproduction—reproduction!"

"The Pall Mall Gazette says that he may soon reach the Treasury Bench."

Sir William was abstracted. He was thinking of that afternoon in Gaston's bedroom, when his grandson had acted, before Lady Dargan and Cluny Vosse, Sir Gaston's scene with Buckingham.

"Really, most mysterious, most unaccountable. But it's one of the virtues of having a descent. When it is most needed, it counts, it counts."

"Against the half-breed mother!" Lady Belward added.

"Quite so, against the—was it Cree or Blackfoot? I've heard him speak of both, but which is in him I do not remember."

"It is very painful; but, poor fellow, it is not his fault, and we ought to be content."

"Indeed, it gives him great originality. Our old families need refreshing now and then."

"Ah, yes, I said so to Mrs. Gasgoyne the other day, and she replied that the refreshment might prove intoxicating. Reine was always rude."

Truth is, Mrs. Gasgoyne was not quite satisfied. That very day she said to her husband:

"You men always stand by each other; but I know you, and you know that I know."

"'Thou knowest the secrets of our hearts'; well, then, you know how we love you. So, be merciful."

"Nonsense, Warren! I tell you he oughtn't to have gone when he did. He has the wild man in him, and I am not satisfied."

"What do you want—me to play the spy?"

"Warren, you're a fool! What do I want? I want the first of September to come quickly, that we may have him with us. With Delia he must go straight. She influences him, he admires her—which is better than mere love. Away from her just now, who can tell what mad adventure—! You see, he has had the curb so long!"

But in a day or two there came a letter-unusually long for Gaston— to Mrs. Gasgoyne herself. It was simple, descriptive, with a dash of epigram. It acknowledged that he had felt the curb, and wanted a touch of the unconventional. It spoke of Ian Belward in a dry phrase, and it asked for the date of the yacht's arrival at Gibraltar.

"Warren, the man is still sensible," she said. "This letter is honest. He is much a heathen at heart, but I believe he hasn't given Delia cause to blush—and that's a good deal! Dear me, I am fond of the fellow— he is so clever. But clever men are trying."

As for Delia, like every sensible English girl, she enjoyed herself in the time of youth, drinking in delightedly the interest attaching to Gaston's betrothed. His letters had been regular, kind yet not emotionally affectionate, interesting, uncommon. He had a knack of saying as much in one page as most people did in five. Her imagination was not great, but he stimulated it. If he wrote a pungent line on Daudet or Whistler, on Montaigne or Fielding, she was stimulated to know them. One day he sent her Whitman's Leaves of Grass, which he had picked up in New York on his way to England. This startled her. She had never heard of Whitman. To her he seemed coarse, incomprehensible, ungentlemanly. She could not understand how Gaston could say beautiful things about Montaigne and about Whitman too. She had no conception how he had in him the strain of that first Sir Gaston Belward, and was also the son of a half-heathen.

He interested her all the more. Her letters were hardly so fascinating to him. She was beautifully correct, but she could not make a sentence breathe. He was grateful, but nothing stirred in him. He could live without her—that he knew regretfully. But he did his part with sincere intention.

That was up to the day when he saw Andree as Mademoiselle Victorine. Then came a swift change. Day after day he visited her, always in the presence of Annette. Soon they dined often together, still in Annette's presence, and the severity of that rule was never relaxed.

Count Ploare came no more; he had received his dismissal. Occasionally Gaston visited the menagerie, but generally after the performance, when Victorine had a half-hour's or an hour's romp with her animals. This was a pleasant time to Gaston. The wild life in him responded.

These were hours when the girl was quite naive and natural, when she spent herself in ripe enjoyment—almost child-like, healthy. At other times there was an indefinable something which Gaston had not noticed in England. But then he had only seen her once. She, too, saw something in him unnoticed before. It was on his tongue a hundred times to tell her that that something was Delia Gasgoyne. He did not. Perhaps because it seemed so grotesque, perhaps because it was easier to drift. Besides, as he said to himself, he would soon go to join the yacht at Gibraltar, and all this would be over-over. All this? All what? A gipsy, a dompteuse —what was she to him? She interested him, he liked her, and she liked him, but there had been nothing more between them. Near as he was to her now, he very often saw her in his mind's eye as she passed over Ridley Common, looking towards him, her eyes shaded by her hand.

She, too, had continually said to herself that this man could be nothing to her—nothing, never! Yet, why not? Count Ploare had offered her his hand. But she knew what had been in Count Ploare's mind. Gaston Belward was different—he had befriended her father. She had not singular scruples regarding men, for she despised most of them. She was not a Mademoiselle Cerise, nor a Madame Juliette, though they were higher on the plane of art than she; or so the world put it. She had not known a man who had not, one time or another, shown himself common or insulting. But since the first moment she had seen Gaston, he had treated her as a lady.

A lady? She had seen enough to smile at that. She knew that she hadn't it in her veins, that she was very much an actress, except in this man's company, when she was mostly natural—as natural as one can be who has a painful secret. They had talked together—for how many hours? She knew exactly. And he had never descended to that which—she felt instinctively—he would not have shown to the ladies of his English world. She knew what ladies were. In her first few weeks in Paris, her fame mounting, she had lunched with some distinguished people, who entertained her as they would have done one of her lions, if that were possible. She understood. She had a proud, passionate nature; she rebelled at this. Invitations were declined at first on pink note-paper with gaudy flowers in a corner, afterwards on cream-laid vellum, when she saw what the great folk did.

And so the days went on, he telling her of his life from his boyhood up —all but the one thing! But that one thing she came to know, partly by instinct, partly by something he accidentally dropped, partly from something Jacques once said to him. Well, what did it matter to her? He would go back; she would remain. It didn't matter.—Yet, why should she lie to herself? It did matter. And why should she care about that girl in England? She was not supposed to know. The other had everything in her favour; what had Andree the gipsy girl, or Mademoiselle Victorine, the dompteuse?

One Sunday evening, after dining together, she asked him to take her to see Saracen. It was a long-standing promise. She had never seen him riding; for their hours did not coincide until the late afternoon or evening. Taking Annette, they went to his new apartments. He had furnished a large studio as a sitting-room, not luxuriantly but pleasantly. It opened into a pretty little garden, with a few plants and trees. They sat there while Jacques went for the horse. Next door a number of students were singing a song of the boulevards. It was followed by one in a woman's voice, sweet and clear and passionate, pitifully reckless. It was, as if in pure contradiction, the opposite of the other—simple, pathetic. At first there were laughing interruptions from the students; but the girl kept on, and soon silence prevailed, save for the voice:

> "And when the wine is dry upon the lip,
> And when the flower is broken by the hand,
> And when I see the white sails of thy ship
> Fly on, and leave me there upon the sand:
> Think you that I shall weep? Nay, I shall smile:
> The wine is drunk, the flower it is gone,
> One weeps not when the days no more beguile,
> How shall the tear-drops gather in a stone?"

When it was ended, Andree, who had listened intently, drew herself up with a little shudder. She sat long, looking into the garden, the cub playing at her feet. Gaston did not disturb her. He got refreshments and put them on the table, rolled a cigarette, and regarded the scene. Her knee was drawn up slightly in her hands, her hat was off, her rich brown hair fell loosely about her head, framing it, her dark eyes glowed under her bent brows. The lion's cub crawled up on the divan, and thrust its nose under an arm. Its head clung to her waist. Who was she? thought Gaston. Delilah, Cleopatra—who? She was lost in thought. She remained so until the garden door opened, and Jacques entered with Saracen.

She looked. Suddenly she came to her feet with a cry of delight, and ran out towards the horse. There was something essentially child-like in her, something also painfully wild-an animal, and a philosopher, and twenty-three.

Jacques put out his hand as he had done with Mademoiselle Cerise.

"No, no; he is savage."

"Nonsense!" she rejoined, and came closer.

Gaston watched, interested. He guessed what she would do.

"A horse!" she added. "Why, you have seen my lions! Leave him free: stand away from him."

Her words were peremptory, and Jacques obeyed. The horse stood alone, a hoof pawing the ground. Presently it sprang away, then half-turned towards the girl, and stood still. She kept talking to him and calling softly, making a coaxing, animal-like sound, as she always did with her lions.

She stepped forward a little and paused. The horse suddenly turned straight towards her, came over slowly, and, with arched neck, dropped his head on her shoulder. She felt the folds of his neck and kissed him. He followed her about the garden like a dog. She brought him to Gaston, locked up, and said with a teasing look, "I have conquered him: he is mine!"

Gaston looked her in her eyes. "He is yours."

"And you?"

"He is mine." His look burned into her soul-how deep, how joyful!

She turned away, her face going suddenly pale. She kept the horse for some time, but at last gave him up again to Jacques. Gaston stepped from the doorway into the garden and met her. It was now dusk. Annette was inside. They walked together in silence for a time. Presently she drew close to him. He felt his veins bounding. Her hand slid into his arm, and, dark as it was, he could see her eyes lifting to his, shining, profound. They had reached the end of the garden, and now turned to come back again.

Suddenly he said, his eyes holding hers: "The horse is yours—and mine."

She stood still; but he could see her bosom heaving hard. She threw up her head with a sound half sob, half laugh. . . .

"You are mad!" she said a moment afterwards, as she lifted her head from his breast.

He laughed softly, catching her cheek to his. "Why be sane? It was to be."

"The gipsy and the gentleman?"

"Gipsies all!"

"And the end of it?"

"Do you not love me, Andree?" She caught her hands over her eyes.

"I do not know what it is—only that it is madness! I see, oh, I see a hundred things."

Her hot eyes were on space. "What do you see?" he urged. She gave a sudden cry:

"I see you at my feet—dead."

"Better than you at mine, Andree."

"Let us go," she said hurriedly.

"Wait," he whispered.

They talked for a little time. Then they entered the studio. Annette was asleep in her chair. Andree waked her, and they bade Gaston good- night.

CHAPTER XVI

WHEREIN LOVE KNOWS NO LAW SAVE THE MAN'S WILL

In another week it was announced that Mademoiselle Victorine would take a month's holiday; to the sorrow of her chief, and to the delight of Mr. Meyerbeer, who had not yet discovered his man, though he had a pretty scandal well-nigh brewed.

Count Ploare was no more, Gaston Belward was. Zoug-Zoug was in the country at Fontainebleau, working at his picture. He had left on the morning after Gaston discovered Andree. He had written, asking his nephew to come for some final sittings. Possibly, he said, Mademoiselle Cerise and others would be down for a Sunday. Gaston had not gone, had briefly declined. His uncle shrugged his shoulders, and went on with other work. It would end in his having to go to Paris and finish the picture there, he said. Perhaps the youth was getting into mischief? So much the better. He took no newspapers.—What did an artist need of them? He did not even read the notices sent by a press-cutting agency. He had a model with him. She amused him for the time, but it was unsatisfactory working on "The King of Ys" from photographs. He loathed it, and gave it up.

One evening Gaston and Andree met at the Gare Montparnasse. Jacques was gone on, but Annette was there. Meyerbeer was there also, at a safe distance. He saw Gaston purchase tickets, arrange his baggage, and enter the train. He passed the compartment, looking in. Besides the three, there was a priest and a young soldier.

Gaston saw him, and guessed what brought him there. He had an impulse to get out and shake him as would Andree's cub a puppy. But the train moved off. Meyerbeer found Gaston's porter. A franc did the business.

"Douarnenez, for Audierne, Brittany," was the legend written in Meyerbeer's note-book. And after that: "Journey twenty hours—change at Rennes, Redon, and Quimpere."

"Too far. I've enough for now," said Meyerbeer, chuckling, as he walked away. "But I'd give five hundred dollars to know who Zoug-Zoug is. I'll make another try."

So he held his sensation back for a while yet. Of the colony at the Hotel St. Malo, not one of the three who knew would tell him. Bagshot had sworn the others to secrecy.

Jacques had gone on with the horses. He was to rent a house, or get rooms at a hotel. He did very well. The horses were stalled at the Hotel de France. He had rented an old chateau perched upon a hill, with steps approaching, steps flanking; near it strange narrow alleys, leading where one cared not to search; a garden of pears and figs, and grapes, and innumerable flowers and an arbour; a pavilion, all windows, over an entranceway, with a shrine in it—a be-starred shrine below it; bare floors, simple furniture, primitiveness at every turn.

Gaston and Andree came, of choice, with a courier in a racketing old diligence from Douarnenez, and they laughed with delight, tired as they were, at the new quarters. It must be a gipsy kind of existence at the most.

There were rooms for Jacques and Annette, who at once set to work with the help of a little Breton maid. Jacques had not ordered a dinner at the hotel, but had got in fresh fish, lobsters, chickens, eggs, and other necessaries; and all was ready for a meal which could be got in an hour.

Jacques had now his hour of happiness. He knew not of these morals— they were beyond him; but after a cheerful dinner in the pavilion, with an omelette made by Andree herself, Annette went to her room and cried herself to sleep. She was civilised, poor soul, and here they were a stone's throw from the cure and the church! Gaston and Andree, refreshed, travelled down the long steps to the village, over the place, along the quay, to the lighthouse and the beach, through crowds of sardine fishers and simple hard-tongued Bretons. Cheerful, buoyant at dinner, there now came upon the girl an intense quiet and fatigue. She stood and looked long at the sea. Gaston tried to rouse her.

"This is your native Brittany, Andree," he said. She pointed far over the sea:

"Near that light at Penmark I was born."

"Can you speak the Breton language?"

"Far worse than you speak Parisian French."

He laughed. "You are so little like these people!"

She had vanity. That had been part of her life. Her beauty had brought trade when she was a gipsy; she had been the admired of Paris: she was only twenty three. Presently she became restless, and shrank from him. Her eyes had a flitting hunted look. Once they met his with a wild sort of pleading or revolt, he could not tell which, and then were continually turned away.

If either could have known how hard the little dwarf of sense and memory was trying to tell her something.

This new phase stunned him. What did it mean? He touched her hand. It was hot, and withdrew from his. He put his arm around her, and she shivered, cringed. But then she was a woman, he thought. He had met one unlike any he had ever known. He would wait. He would be patient. Would she come—home? She turned passively and took his arm. He talked, but he knew he was talking poorly, and at last he became silent also. But when they came to the steep steps leading to the chateau, he lifted her in his arms, carried her to the house, and left her at their chamber- door.

Then he went to the pavilion to smoke. He had no wish to think— at least of anything but the girl. It was not a time for retrospect, but to accept a situation. The die had been cast. He had followed what —his nature, his instincts? The consequence?

He heard Andree's voice. He went to her.

The next morning they were in the garden walking about. They had been speaking, but now both were silent. At last he turned again to her.

"Andree, who was the other man?" he asked quietly, but with a strange troubled look in his eyes.

She shrank away confused, a kind of sickness in her eyes.

"What does it matter?" she said.

"Of course, of course," he returned in a low, nerveless tone.

They were silent for a long time. Meanwhile, she seemed to beat up a feverish cheerfulness. At last she said:

"Where do we go this afternoon, Gaston?"

"We will see," he replied.

The day passed, another, and another. The same: she shrank from him, was impatient, agitated, unhappy, went out alone. Annette saw, and mourned, entreated, prayed; Jacques was miserable. There was no joyous passion to redeem the situation for which Gaston had risked so much.

They rode, they took excursions in fishing-boats and little sail-boats. Andree entered into these with zest: talked to the sailors, to Jacques, caressed children, and was not indifferent to the notice she attracted in the village; but was obviously distrait. Gaston was patient—and unhappy. So, this was the merchandise for which he had bartered all! But he had a will, he was determined; he had sowed, he would reap his harvest to the useless stubble.

"Do you wish to go back to your work?" he said quietly, once.

"I have no work," she answered apathetically. He said no more just then.

The days and weeks went by. The situation was impossible, not to be understood. Gaston made his final move. He hoped that perhaps a forced crisis might bring about a change. If it failed—he knew not what! She was sitting in the garden below—he alone in the window, smoking. A bundle of letters and papers, brought by the postman that evening, were beside him.

He would not open them yet. He felt that there was trouble in them—he saw phrases, sentences flitting past him. But he would play this other bitter game out first. He let them lie. He heard the bells in the church ringing the village commerce done—it was nine o'clock. The picture of that other garden in Paris came to him: that night when he had first taken this girl into his arms. She sat below talking to Annette and singing a little Breton chanson:

"Parvondt varbondt anan oun,
Et die don la lire!
Parvondt varbondt anan oun,
Et die don la, la!"

He called down to her presently. "Andree!"

"Yes."

"Will you come up for a moment, please?"

"Surely."

She came up, leaving the room door open, and bringing the cub with her.

He called Jacques.

"Take the cub to its quarters, Jacques," he said, quietly.

She seemed about to protest, but sat back and watched him. He shut the door—locked it. Then he came and sat down before her.

"Andree," he said, "this is all impossible."

"What is impossible?"

"You know well. I am not a mere brute. The only thing that can redeem this life is love."

"That is true," she said, coldly. "What then?"

"You do not redeem it. We must part."

She laughed fitfully. "We must—?"

She leaned towards him.

"To-morrow evening you will go back to Paris. To-night we part, however: that is, our relations cease."

"I shall go from here when it pleases me, Gaston!"

His voice came low and stern, but courteous:

"You must go when I tell you. Do you think I am the weaker?"

He could see her colour flying, her fingers lacing and interlacing.

"Aren't you afraid to tell me that?" she asked.

"Afraid? Of my life—you mean that? That you will be as common as that? No: you will do as I tell you."

He fixed his eyes on hers, and held them. She sat, looking. Presently she tried to take her eyes away. She could not. She shuddered and shrank.

He withdrew his eyes for a moment. "You will go?" he asked.

"It makes no difference," she answered; then added sharply: "Who are you, to look at me like that, to—!"

She paused.

"I am your friend and your master!"

He rose. "Good-night," he said, at the door, and went out.

He heard the key turn in the lock. He had forgotten his papers and letters. It did not matter. He would read them when she was gone—if she did go. He was far from sure that he had succeeded. He went to bed in another room, and was soon asleep.

He was waked in the very early morning by feeling a face against his, wet, trembling.

"What is it, Andree?" he asked. Her arms ran round his neck.

"Oh, mon amour! Mon adore! Je t'aime! Je t'aime!"

In the evening of this day she said she knew not how it was, but on that first evening in Audierne there suddenly came to her a strange terrible feeling, which seemed to dry up all the springs of her desire for him. She could not help it. She had fought against it, but it was no use; yet she knew that she could not leave him. After he had told her to go, she had had a bitter struggle: now tears, now anger, and a wish to hate. At last she fell asleep. When she awoke she had changed, she was her old self, as in Paris, when she had first confessed her love. She felt that she must die if she did not go to him. All the first passion returned, the passion that began on the common at Ridley Court. "And now—now," she said, "I know that I cannot live without you."

It seemed so. Her nature was emptying itself. Gaston had got the merchandise for which he had given a price yet to be known.

"You asked me of the other man," she said. "I will tell you."

"Not now," he said. "You loved him?"

"No—ah God, no!" she answered.

An hour after, when she was in her room, he opened the little bundle of correspondence.—A memorandum with money from his bankers. A letter from Delia, and also one from Mrs. Gasgoyne, saying that they expected to meet him at Gibraltar on a certain day, and asking why he had not written; Delia with sorrowful reserve, Mrs. Gasgoyne with impatience. His letters had missed them—he had written on leaving Paris, saying that his plans were indefinite, but he would write them definitely soon. After he came to Audierne it seemed impossible to write. How could he? No, let the American journalist do it. Better so. Better himself in the worst light, with the full penalty, than his own confession—in itself an insult. So it had gone on. He slowly tore up the letters. The next were from his grandfather and grandmother—they did not know yet. He could not read them. A few loving sentences, and then he said:

"What's the good! Better not." He tore them up also. Another—from his uncle. It was brief:

You've made a sweet mess of it, Cadet. It's in all the papers to- day. Meyerbeer telegraphed it to New York and London. I'll probably come down to see you. I want to finish my picture on the site of the old City of Ys, there at Point du Raz. Your girl can pose with you. I'll do all I can to clear the thing up. But a British M.P.—that's a tough pill for Clapham!

Gaston's foot tapped the floor angrily. He scattered the pieces of the letter at his feet. Now for the newspapers. He opened Le Petit Journal, Coil Blas, Galignani, and the New York Tom-Tom, one by one. Yes, it was there, with pictures of himself and Andree. A screaming sensation. Extracts, too, from the English papers by telegram. He read them all unflinchingly. There was one paragraph which he did not understand:

There was a previous friend of the lady, unknown to the public, called Zoug-Zoug.

He remembered that day at the Hotel St. Malo! Well, the bolt was shot: the worst was over. Quid refert? Justify himself?

Certainly, to all but Delia Gasgoyne.

Thousands of men did the same—did it in cold blood, without one honest feeling. He did it, at least under a powerful influence. He could not help but smile now at the thought of how he had filled both sides of the equation. On his father's side, bringing down the mad record from Naseby; on his mother's, true to the heathen, by following his impulses —sacred to primitive man, justified by spear, arrow, and a strong arm. Why sheet home this as a scandal? How did they—the libellers—know but that he had married the girl? Exactly. He would see to that. He would play his game with open sincerity now. He could have wished secrecy for Delia Gasgoyne, and for his grandfather and grandmother,—he was not wilfully brutal,—but otherwise he had no shame at all; he would stand openly for his right. Better one honest passion than a life of deception and miserable compromise. A British M.P.?—He had thrown away his reputation, said the papers. By this? The girl was no man's wife, he was no woman's husband!

Marry her? Yes, he would marry her; she should be his wife. His people? It was a pity. Poor old people—they would fret and worry. He had been selfish, had not thought of them? Well, who could foresee this outrage of journalism? The luck had been dead against him. Did he not know plenty of men in London—he was going to say the Commons, but he was fairer to the Commons than it, as a body, would be to him—who did much worse? These had escaped: the hunters had been after him. What would he do? Take the whip? He got to his feet with an oath. Take the whip? Never—never! He would fight this thing tooth and nail. Had he come to England to let them use him for a sensation only—a sequence of surprises, to end in a tragedy, all for the furtive pleasure of the British breakfast-table? No, by the Eternal! What had the first Gaston done? He had fought—fought Villiers and others, and had held up his head beside his King and Rupert till the hour of Naseby.

When the summer was over he would return to Paris, to London. The journalist—punish him? No; too little—a product of his time. But the British people he would fight, and he would not give up Ridley Court. He could throw the game over when it was all his, but never when it was going dead against him.

That speech in the Commons? He remembered gladly that he had contended for conceptions of social miseries according to surrounding influences of growth and situation. He had not played the hypocrite.

No, not even with Delia. He had acted honestly at the beginning, and afterwards he had done what he could so long as he could. It was inevitable that she must be hurt, even if he had married, not giving her what he had given this dompteuse. After all, was it so terrible? It could not affect her much in the eyes of the world. And her heart? He did not flatter himself. Yet he knew that it would be the thing—the fallen idol—that would grieve her more than thought of the man. He wished that he could have spared her in the circumstances. But it had all come too suddenly: it was impossible. He had spared, he could spare, nobody. There was the whole situation. What now to do?—To remain here while it pleased them, then Paris, then London for his fight.

Three days went round. There were idle hours by the sea, little excursions in a sail-boat to Penmark, and at last to Point du Raz. It was a beautiful day, with a gentle breeze, and the point was glorified. The boat ran in lightly between the steep dark shore and the comb of reef that looked like a host of stealthy pumas crumbling the water. They anchored in the Bay des Trepasses. An hour on shore exploring the caves, and lunching, and then they went back to the boat, accompanied by a Breton sailor, who had acted as guide.

Gaston lay reading,—they were in the shade of the cliff,—while Andree listened to the Breton tell the legends of the coast. At length Gaston's attention was attracted. The old sailor was pointing to the shore, and speaking in bad French.

"Voila, madame, where the City of Ys stood long before the Bretons came. It was a foolish ride."

"I do not know the story. Tell me."

"There are two or three, but mine is the oldest. A flood came—sent by the gods, for the woman was impious. The king must ride with her into the sea and leave her there, himself to come back, and so save the city."

The sailor paused to scan the sea—something had struck him. He shook his head. Gaston was watching Andree from behind his book.

"Well, well," she said, impatiently, "what then? What did he do?"

"The king took up the woman, and rode into the water as far as where you see the great white stone—it has been there ever since. There he had a fight—not with the woman, but in his heart. He turned to the people, and cried: 'Dry be your streets, and as ashes your eyes for your king!' And then he rode on with the woman till they saw him no more—never!" Andree said instantly:

"That was long ago. Now the king would ride back alone."

She did not look at Gaston, but she knew that his eyes were on her. He closed the book, got up, came forward to the sailor, who was again looking out to sea, and said carelessly over his shoulder:

"Men who lived centuries ago would act the same now, if they were here."

Her response seemed quite as careless as his: "How do you know?"

"Perhaps I had an innings then," he answered, smiling whimsically.

She was about to speak again, but the guide suddenly said:

"You must get away. There'll be a change of wind and a bad cross-current soon."

In a few minutes the two were bearing out—none too soon, for those pumas crowded up once or twice within a fathom of their deck, devilish and devouring. But they wore away with a capricious current, and down a tossing sea made for Audierne.

CHAPTER XVII

THE MAN AND THE WOMAN FACE THE INTOLERABLE

In a couple of hours they rounded Point de Leroily, and ran for the harbour. By hugging the quay in the channel to the left of the bar, they were sure of getting in, though the tide was low. The boat was docile to the lug-sail and the helm. As they were beating in they saw a large yacht running straight across a corner of the bar for the channel. It was Warren Gasgoyne's Kismet.

The Kismet had put into Audierne rather than try to pass Point du Raz at night. At Gibraltar a telegram had come telling of the painful sensation, and the yacht was instantly headed for England; Mrs. Gasgoyne crossing the Continent, Delia preferring to go back with her father—his sympathy was more tender. They had seen no newspapers, and they did not know that Gaston was at Audierne. Gasgoyne knowing, as all the world knew, that there was a bar at the mouth of the harbour, allowed himself, as he thought, sufficient room, but the wind had suddenly drawn ahead, and he was obliged to keep away. Presently the yacht took the ground with great force.

Gasgoyne put the helm hard down, but she would not obey. He tried at once to get in his sails, but the surf was running very strong, and presently a heavy sea broke clean over her. Then came confusion and dismay: the flapping of the wet, half-lowered sails, and the whipping of the slack ropes, making all effort useless. There was no chance of her- holding. Foot by foot she was being driven towards the rocks. Sailors stood motionless on the shore. The lifeboat would be of little use: besides, it could not arrive for some time.

Gaston had recognised the Kismet. He turned to Andree.

"There's danger, but perhaps we can do it. Will you go?"

She flushed.

"Have I ever been a coward, Gaston? Tell me what to do."

"Keep the helm firm, and act instantly on my orders."

Instead of coming round into the channel, he kept straight on past the lighthouse towards the yacht, until he was something to seaward of her. Then, luffing quickly, he dropped sail, let go the anchor, and unshipped the mast, while Andree got the oars into the rowlocks. It was his idea to dip under the yacht's stern, but he found himself drifting alongside, and in danger of dashing broadside on her. He got an oar and backed with all his strength towards the stern, the anchor holding well. Then he called to those on board to be ready to jump. Once in line with the Kismet's counter, he eased off the painter rapidly, and now dropped towards the stern of the wreck.

Gaston was quite cool. He did not now think of the dramatic nature of this meeting, apart from the physical danger. Delia also had recognised him, and guessed who the girl was. Not to respond to Gaston's call was her first instinct. But then, life was sweet. Besides, she had to think of others. Her father, too, was chiefly concerned for her safety and for his yacht. He had almost determined to get Delia on Gaston's boat, and himself take the chances with the Kismet; but his sailors dissuaded him, declaring that the chances were against succour.

The only greetings were words of warning and direction from Gaston. Presently there was an opportunity. Gaston called sharply to Delia, and she, standing ready, jumped. He caught her in his arms as she came. The boat swayed as the others leaped, and he held her close meanwhile. Her eyes closed, she shuddered and went white. When he put her down, she covered her face with her hands, trembling. Then, suddenly she came huddling in a heap, and burst into tears.

They slipped the painter, a sailor took Andree's place at the helm, the oars were got out, and they made over to the channel, grazing the bar once or twice, by reason of the now heavy load.

Warren Gasgoyne and Gaston had not yet spoken in the way of greeting. The former went to Delia now and said a few cheery words, but, from behind her handkerchief, she begged him to leave her alone for a moment.

"Nerves, all nerves, Mr. Belward," he said, turning towards Gaston. "But, then, it was ticklish-ticklish."

They did not shake hands. Gaston was looking at Delia, and he did not reply.

Mr. Gasgoyne continued:

"Nasty sea coming on—afraid to try Point du Raz. Of course we didn't know you were here."

He looked at Andree curiously. He was struck by the girl's beauty and force. But how different from Delia!

He suddenly turned, and said bluntly, in a low voice: "Belward, what a fool—what a fool! You had it all at your feet: the best—the very best."

Gaston answered quietly:

"It's an awkward time for talking. The rocks will have your yacht in half an hour."

Gasgoyne turned towards it.

"Yes, she'll get a raking fore and aft." Then, he added, suddenly: "Of course you know how we feel about our rescue. It was plucky of you."

"Pluckier in the girl," was the reply. "Brave enough," the honest rejoinder.

Gaston had an impulse to say, "Shall I thank her for you?" but he was conscious how little right he had to be ironical with Warren Gasgoyne, and he held his peace.

While the two were now turned away towards the Kismet, Andree came to Delia. She did not quite know how to comfort her, but she was a woman, and perhaps a supporting arm would do something.

"There, there," she said, passing a hand round her shoulder, "you are all right now. Don't cry!"

With a gasp of horror, Delia got to her feet, but swayed, and fell fainting—into Andree's arms.

She awoke near the landing-place, her father beside her. Meanwhile Andree had read the riddle. As Mr. Gasgoyne bathed Delia's face, and Gaston her wrists, and gave her brandy, she sat still and intent, watching. Tears and fainting! Would she—Andree-have given way like that in the same circumstances? No. But this girl—Delia—was of a different order: was that it? All nerves and sentiment! At one of those lunches in the grand world she had seen a lady burst into tears suddenly at some one's reference to Senegal. She herself had only cried four times, that she remembered; when her mother died; when her father was called a thief; when, one day, she suffered the first great shame of her life in the mountains of Auvergne; and the night when she waked a second time to her love for Gaston. She dared to call it love, though good Annette had called it a mortal sin.

What was to be done? The other woman must suffer.

The man was hers—hers for ever. He had said it: for ever. Yet her heart had a wild hunger for that something which this girl had and she had not. But the man was hers; she had won him away from this other.

Delia came upon the quay bravely, passing through the crowd of staring fishermen, who presently gave Gaston a guttural cheer. Three of them, indeed, had been drinking his health. They embraced him and kissed him, begging him to come with them for absinthe. He arranged the matter with a couple of francs.

Then he wondered what now was to be done. He could not insult the Gasgoynes by asking them to come to the chateau. He proposed the Hotel de France to Mr. Gasgoyne, who assented. It was difficult to separate here on the quay: they must all walk together to the hotel. Gaston turned to speak to Andree, but she was gone. She had saved the situation.

The three spoke little, and then but formally, as they walked to the hotel. Mr. Gasgoyne said that they would leave by train for Paris the next day, going to Douarnenez that evening. They had saved nothing from the yacht.

Delia did not speak. She was pale, composed now. In the hotel Mr. Gasgoyne arranged for rooms, while Gaston got some sailors together, and, in Mr. Gasgoyne's name, offered a price for the recovery of the yacht or of certain things in her. Then he went into the hotel to see if he could do anything further. The door of the sitting-room was open, and no answer coming to his knock, he entered.

Delia was standing in the window. Against her will her father had gone to find a doctor. Gaston would have drawn back if she had not turned round wearily to him.

Perhaps it were well to get it over now. He came forward. She made no motion.

"I hope you feel better?" he said. "It was a bad accident."

"I am tired and shaken, of course," she responded. "It was very brave of you."

He hesitated, then said:

"We were more fortunate than brave."

He was determined to have Andree included. She deserved that; the wrong to Delia was not hers.

But she answered after the manner of a woman: "The girl—ah, yes, please thank her for us. What is her name?"

"She is known in Audierne as Madame Belward." The girl started. Her face had a cold, scornful pride. "The Bretons, then, have a taste for fiction?"

"No, they speak as they are taught."

"They understand, then, as little as I."

How proud, how ineffaceably superior she was!

"Be ignorant for ever," he answered quietly.

"I do not need the counsel, believe me."

Her hand trembled, though it rested against the window-trembled with indignation: the insult of his elopement kept beating up her throat in spite of her.

At that moment a servant knocked, entered, and said that a parcel had been brought for mademoiselle. It was laid upon the table. Delia, wondering, ordered it to be opened. A bundle of clothes was disclosed— Andree's! Gaston recognised them, and caught his breath with wonder and confusion.

"Who has sent them?" Delia said to the servant. "They come from the Chateau Ronan, mademoiselle."

Delia dismissed the servant.

"The Chateau Ronan?" she asked of Gaston. "Where I am living."

"It is not necessary to speak of this?" She flushed.

"Not at all. I will have them sent back. There is a little shop near by where you can get what you may need."

Andree had acted according to her lights. It was not an olive-branch, but a touch of primitive hospitality. She was Delia's enemy at sight, but a woman must have linen.

Mr. Gasgoyne entered. Gaston prepared to go. "Is there anything more that I can do?" he said, as it were, to both.

The girl replied. "Nothing at all, thank you." They did not shake hands.

Mr. Gasgoyne could not think that all had necessarily ended. The thing might be patched up one day yet. This affair with the dompteuse was mad sailing, but the man might round-to suddenly and be no worse for the escapade.

"We are going early in the morning," he said. "We can get along all right. Good-bye. When do you come to England?"

The reply was prompt. "In a few weeks."

He looked at both. The girl, seeing that he was going to speak further, bowed and left the room.

His eyes followed her. After a moment, he said firmly

"Mr. Gasgoyne, I am going to face all."

"To live it down, Belward?"

"I am going to fight it down."

"Well, there's a difference. You have made a mess of things, and shocked us all. I needn't say what more. It's done, and now you know what such things mean to a good woman—and, I hope also, to the father of a good woman."

The man's voice broke a little. He added:

"They used to come to swords or pistols on such points. We can't settle it in that way. Anyhow, you have handicapped us to-day." Then, with a burst of reproach, indignation, and trouble: "Great God, as if you hadn't been the luckiest man on earth! Delia, the estate, the Commons—all for a dompteuse!"

"Let us say nothing more," said Gaston, choking down wrath at the reference to Andree, but sorrowful, and pitying Mr. Gasgoyne. Besides, the man had a right to rail.

Soon after they parted courteously.

Gaston went to the chateau. As he came up the stone steps he met a procession—it was the feast-day of the Virgin—of priests and people and little children, filing up from the village and the sea, singing as they came. He drew up to the wall, stood upon the stone seat, and took off his hat while the procession passed. He had met the cure, first accidentally on the shore, and afterwards in the cure's house, finding much in common—he had known many priests in the North, known much good of them. The cure glanced up at him now as they passed, and a half-sad smile crossed his face. Gaston caught it as it passed. The cure read his case truly enough and gently enough too. In some wise hour he would plead with Gaston for the woman's soul and his own.

Gaston did not find Andree at the chateau. She had gone out alone towards the sea, Annette said, by a route at the rear of the village. He went also, but did not find her. As he came again to the quay he saw the Kismet beating upon the rocks—the sailors had given up any idea of saving her. He stood and watched the sea breaking over her, and the whole scene flashed back on him. He thought how easily he could be sentimental over the thing. But that was not his nature. He had made his bed, but he would not lie in it—he would carry it on his back. They all said that he had gone on the rocks. He laughed.

"I can turn that tide: I can make things come my way," he said. "All they want is sensation, it isn't morals that concerns them. Well, IT give them sensation. They expect me to hide, and drop out of the game. Never—so help me Heaven! I'll play it so they'll forget this!"

He rolled and lighted a cigarette, and went again to the chateau. Dinner was ready—had been ready for some time. He sat down, and presently Andree came. There was a look in her face that he could not understand. They ate their dinner quietly, not mentioning the events of the afternoon.

Presently a telegram was brought to him. It read: "Come. My office, Downing Street, Friday. Expect you." It was signed "Faramond." At the same time came letters: from his grandfather, from Captain Maudsley. The first was stern, imperious, reproachful.—Shame for those that took him in and made him, a ruined reputation, a spoiled tradition: he had been but a heathen after all! There was only left to bid him farewell, and to enclose a cheque for two thousand pounds.

Captain Maudsley called him a fool, and asked him what he meant to do —hoped he would give up the woman at once, and come back. He owed something to his position as Master of the Hounds—a tradition that oughtn't to be messed about.

There it all was: not a word about radical morality or immorality; but the tradition of Family, the Commons, Master of the Hounds!

But there was another letter. He did not recognise the handwriting, and the envelope had a black edge. He turned it over and over, forgetting that Andree was watching him. Looking up, he caught her eyes, with their strange, sad look. She guessed what was in these letters. She knew English well enough to under stand them. He interpreted her look, and pushed them over.

"You may read them, if you wish; but I wouldn't, if I were you."

She read the telegram first, and asked who "Faramond" was. Then she read Sir William Belward's letter, and afterwards Captain Maudsley's.

"It has all come at once," she said: "the girl and these! What will you do? Give 'the woman' up for the honour of the Master of the Hounds?"

The tone was bitter, exasperating. Gaston was patient.

"What do you think, Andree?"

"It has only begun," she said. "Wait, King of Ys. Read that other letter."

Her eyes were fascinated by the black border. He opened it with a strange slowness. It began without any form of address, it had the superscription of a street in Manchester Square:

If you were not in deep trouble I would not write. But because I know that more hard things than kind will be said by others, I want to say what is in my heart, which is quick to feel for you. I know that you have sinned, but I pray for you every day, and I cannot believe that God will not answer. Oh! think of the wrong that you have done: of the wrong to the girl, to her soul's good. Think of that, and right the wrong in so far as you can. Oh, Gaston, my brother, I need not explain why I write thus. My grandfather, before he died, three weeks ago, told me that you know!—and I also have known ever since the day you saved the boy. Ah, think of one who would give years of her life to see you good and noble and happy. . . .

Then followed a deep, sincere appeal to his manhood, and afterwards a wish that their real relations should be made known to the world if he needed her, or if disaster came; that she might share and comfort his life, whatever it might be. Then again:

If you love her, and she loves you, and is sorry for what she has done, marry her and save her from everlasting shame. I am staying with my grandfather's cousin, the Dean of Dighbury, the father of the boy you saved. He is very kind, and he knows all. May God guide you aright, and may you believe that no one speaks more truthfully to you than your sorrowful and affectionate sister,

ALICE WINGFIELD.

He put the letter down beside him, made a cigarette, and poured out some coffee for them both. He was holding himself with a tight hand. This letter had touched him as nothing in his life had done since his father's death. It had nothing of noblesse oblige, but straight statement of wrong, as she saw it. And a sister without an open right to the title: the mere fidelity of blood! His father had brought this sorrowful life into the world and he had made it more sorrowful—poor little thing—poor girl!

"What are you going to do?" asked Andree. "Do you go back—with Delia?"

He winced. Yet why should he expect of her too great refinement? She had not had a chance, she had not the stuff for it in her veins; she had never been taught. But behind it all was her passion—her love—for him.

"You know that's altogether impossible!" he answered.

"She would not take you back."

"Probably not. She has pride."

"Pride-chat! She'd jump at the chance!"

"That sounds rude, Andree; and it is contradictory."

"Rude! Well, I'm only a gipsy and a dompteuse!"

"Is that all, my girl?"

"That's all, now." Then, with a sudden change and a quick sob: "But I may be— Oh, I can't say it, Gaston!" She hid her face for a moment on his shoulder. "My God!"

He got to his feet. He had not thought of that—of another besides themselves. He had drifted. A hundred ideas ran back and forth. He went to the window and stood looking out. Alice's letter was still in his fingers.

She came and touched his shoulder.

"Are you going to leave me, Gaston? What does that letter say?"

He looked at her kindly, with a protective tenderness.

"Read the letter, Andree," he said.

She did so, at first slowly, then quickly, then over and over again. He stood motionless in the window. She pushed the letter between his fingers. He did not turn. "I cannot understand everything, but what she says she means. Oh, Gaston, what a fool, what a fool you've been!"

After a moment, however, she threw her arms about him with animal-like fierceness.

"But I can't give you up—I can't." Then, with another of those sudden changes, she added, with a wild little laugh: "I can't, I can't, O Master of the Hounds!"

There came a knock at the door. Annette entered with a letter. The postman had not delivered it on his rounds, because the address was not correct. It was for madame. Andree took it, started at the handwriting, tore open the envelope, and read:

Zoug-Zoug congratulates you on the conquest of his nephew. Zoug- Zoug's name is not George Maur, as you knew him. Allah's blessing, with Zoug-Zoug's!

What fame you've got now—dompteuse, and the sweet scandal!

The journalist had found out Zoug-Zoug at last, and Ian Belward had talked with the manager of the menagerie.

Andree shuddered and put the letter in her pocket. Now she understood why she had shrunk from Gaston that first night and those first days in Audierne: that strange sixth sense, divination—vague, helpless prescience. And here, suddenly, she shrank again, but with a different thought. She hurriedly left the room and went to her chamber.

In a few moments he came to her. She was sitting upright in a chair, looking straight before her. Her lips were bloodless, her eyes were burning. He came and took her hands.

"What is it, Andree?" he said. "That letter, what is it?"

She looked at him steadily. "You'll be sorry if you read it." But she gave it to him. He lighted a candle, put it on a little table, sat down, and read. The shock went deep; so deep that it made no violent sign on the surface. He spread the letter out before him. The candle showed his face gone grey and knotted with misery. He could bear all the rest: fight, do all that was right to the coming mother of his child; but this made him sick and dizzy. He felt as he did when he waked up in Labrador, with his wife's dead lips pressed to his neck. It was strange too that Andree was as quiet as he: no storm-misery had gone deep with her also.

"Do you care to tell me about it?" he asked.

She sat back in her chair, her hands over her eyes. Presently, still sitting so, she spoke.

Ian Belward had painted them and their van in the hills of Auvergne, and had persuaded her to sit for a picture. He had treated her courteously at first. Her father was taken ill suddenly, and died. She was alone for a few days afterwards. Ian Belward came to her. Of that miserable, heart-rending, cruel time,—the life-sorrow of a defenceless girl,— Gaston heard with a hard sort of coldness. The promised marriage was a matter for the man's mirth a week later. They came across three young artists from Paris—Bagshot, Fancourt, and another—who camped one night beside them. It was then she fully realised the deep shame of her position. The next night she ran away and joined a travelling menagerie. The rest he knew. When she had ended there was silence for a time, broken only by one quick gasping sob from Gaston. The girl sat still as death, her eyes on him intently.

"Poor Andree! Poor girl!" he said at last. She sighed pitifully.

"What shall we do?" she asked. He scarcely spoke above a whisper:

"There must be time to think. I will go to London."

"You will come back?"

"Yes—in five days, if I live."

"I believe you," she said quietly. "You never lied to me. When you return we will know what to do." Her manner was strangely quiet. "A little trading schooner goes from Douarnenez to England to-morrow morning," she went on. "There is a notice of it in the market-place. That would save the journey to Paris.'"

"Yes, that will do very well. I will start for Douarnenez at once."

"Will Jacques go too?"

"No."

An hour later he passed Delia and her father on the road to Douarnenez. He did not recognise them, but Delia, seeing him, shrank away in a corner of the carriage, trembling.

Jacques had wished to go to London with Gaston, but had been denied. He was to care for the horses. When he saw his master ride down over the place, waving a hand back towards him, he came in and said to Andree:

"Madame, there is trouble—I do not know what. But I once said I would never leave him, wherever he go or whatever he did. Well, I never will leave him—or you, madame—no."

"That is right, that is right," she said earnestly; "you must never leave him, Jacques. He is a good man."

When Jacques had gone she shut herself up in her room. She was gathering all her life into the compass of an hour. She felt but one thing: the ruin of her happiness and Gaston's.

"He is a good man," she said over and over to herself. And the other—Ian Belward? All the barbarian in her was alive.

The next morning she started for Paris, saying to Jacques and Annette that she would return in four days.

CHAPTER XVIII

"RETURN, O SHULAMITE!"

Almost the first person that Gaston recognised in London was Cluny Vosse. He had been to Victoria Station to see a friend off by the train, and as he was leaving, Gaston and he recognised each other. The lad's greeting was a little shy until he saw that Gaston was cool and composed as usual —in effect, nothing had happened. Cluny was delighted, and opened his mind:

"They'd kicked up a deuce of a row in the papers, and there'd been no end of talk; but he didn't see what all the babble was about, and he'd said so again and again to Lady Dargan."

"And Lady Dargan, Cluny?" asked Gaston quietly. Cluny could not be dishonest, though he would try hard not to say painful things.

"Well, she was a bit fierce at first—she's a woman, you know; but afterwards she went like a baby; cried, and wouldn't stay at Cannes any longer: so we're back in town. We're going down to the country, though, to-morrow or next day."

"Do you think I had better call, Cluny?" Gaston ventured suggestively.

"Yes, yes, of course," Cluny replied, with great eagerness, as if to justify the matter to himself. Gaston smiled, said that he might,— he was only in town for a few days, and dropped Cluny in Pall Mall. Cluny came running back.

"I say, Belward, things'll come around just as they were before, won't they? You're going to cut in, and not let 'em walk on you?"

"Yes, I'm 'going to cut in,' Cluny boy." Cluny brightened.

"And of course it isn't all over with Delia, is it?" He blushed.

Gaston reached out and dropped a hand on Cluny's shoulder.

"I'm afraid it is all over, Cluny." Cluny spoke without thinking.

"I say, it's rough on her, isn't it?"

Then he was confused, hurriedly offered Gaston a cigarette, a hasty good-bye was said, and they parted. Gaston went first to Lord Faramond. He encountered inquisition, cynical humour, flashes of sympathy, with a general flavour of reproach. The tradition of the Commons! Ah, one way only: he must come back alone—alone—and live it down. Fortunately, it wasn't an intrigue—no matter of divorce—a dompteuse, he believed. It must end, of course, and he would see what could be done. Such a chance —such a chance as he had had! Make it up with his grandfather, and reverse the record—reverse the record: that was the only way. This meeting must, of course, be strictly between themselves. But he was really interested for him, for his people, and for the tradition of the Commons.

"I am Master of the Hounds too," said Gaston dryly. Lord Faramond caught the meaning, and smiled grimly.

Then came Gaston's decision—he would come back—not to live the thing down, but to hold his place as long as he could: to fight.

Lord Faramond shrugged a shoulder. "Without her?"

"I cannot say that."

"With her, I can promise nothing—nothing. You cannot fight it so. No one man is stronger than massed opinion. It is merely a matter of pressure. No, no; I can promise nothing in that case."

The Premier's face had gone cold and disdainful. Why should a clever man like Belward be so infatuated? He rose, Gaston thanked him for the meeting, and was about to go, when the Prime Minister, tapping his shoulder kindly, said:

"Mr. Belward, you are not playing to the rules of the game." He waved his hand towards the Chamber of the House. "It is the greatest game in the world. She must go! Do not reply. You will come back without her —good-bye!"

Then came Ridley Court. He entered on Sir William and Lady Belward without announcement. Sir William came to his feet, austere and pale. Lady Belward's fingers trembled on the lace she held. They looked many years older. Neither spoke his name, nor did they offer their hands. Gaston did not wince, he had expected it. He owed these old people something. They lived according to their lights, they had acted righteously as by their code, they had used him well—well always.

"Will you hear the whole story?" he said. He felt that it would be best to tell them all. "Can it do any good?" asked Sir William. He looked towards his wife.

"Perhaps it is better to hear it," she murmured. She was clinging to a vague hope.

Gaston told the story plainly, briefly, as he had told his earlier history. Its concision and simplicity were poignant. From the day he first saw Andree in the justice's room till the hour when she opened Ian Belward's letter, his tale went. Then he paused.

"I remember very well," Sir William said, with painful meditation: "a strange girl, with a remarkable face. You pleaded for her father then. Ah, yes, an unhappy case!"

"There is more?" asked Lady Belward, leaning on her cane. She seemed very frail.

Then with a terrible brevity Gaston told them of his uncle, of the letter to Andree: all, except that Andree was his wife. He had no idea of sparing Ian Belward now. A groan escaped Lady Belward.

"And now—now, what will you do?" asked the baronet.

"I do not know. I am going back first to Andree." Sir William's face was ashy.

"Impossible!"

"I promised, and I will go back." Lady Belward's voice quivered:

"Stay, ah, stay, and redeem the past! You can, you can outlive it."

Always the same: live it down!

"It is no use," he answered; "I must return."

Then in a few words he thanked them for all, and bade them good-bye. He did not offer his hand, nor did they. But at the door he heard Lady Belward say in a pleading voice:

"Gaston!"

He returned. She held out her hand.

"You must not do as your father did," she said. "Give the woman up, and come back to us. Am I nothing to you—nothing?"

"Is there no other way?" he asked, gravely, sorrowfully.

She did not reply. He turned to his grandfather. "There is no other way," said the old man, sternly. Then in a voice almost shrill with pain and indignation, he cried out as he had never done in his life: "Nothing, nothing, nothing but disgrace! My God in heaven! a lion-tamer—a gipsy! An honourable name dragged through the mire! Go back," he said grandly; "go back to the woman and her lions—savages, savages, savages!"

"Savages after the manner of our forefathers," Gaston answered quietly. "The first Gaston showed us the way. His wife was a strolling player's daughter. Good-bye, sir."

Lady Belward's face was in her hands. "Good-bye-grandmother," he said at the door, and then he was gone.

At the outer door the old housekeeper stepped forward, her gloomy face most agitated.

"Oh, sir, oh, sir, you will come back again? Oh, don't go like your father!"

He suddenly threw an arm about her shoulder, and kissed her on the cheek.

"I'll come back—yes I'll come back here—if I can. Good-bye, Hovey."

In the library Sir William and Lady Belward sat silent for a time. Presently Sir William rose, and walked up and down. He paused at last, and said, in a strange, hesitating voice, his hands chafing each other:

"I forgot myself, my dear. I fear I was violent. I would like to ask his pardon. Ah, yes, yes!"

Then he sat down and took her hand, and held it long in the silence.

"It all feels so empty—so empty," she said at last, as the tower-clock struck hollow on the air.

The old man could not reply, but he drew her close to him, and Hovey, from the door, saw his tears dropping on her white hair.

Gaston went to Manchester Square. He half dreaded a meeting with Alice, and yet he wished it. He did not find her. She had gone to Paris with her uncle, the servant said. He got their address. There was little left to do but to avoid reporters, two of whom almost forced themselves in upon him. He was to go back to Douarnenez by the little boat that brought him, and at seven o'clock in the morning he watched the mists of England recede.

He chanced to put his hand into a light overcoat which he had got at his chambers before he started. He drew out a paper, the one discovered in the solicitor's office in London. It was an ancient deed of entail of the property, drawn by Sir Gaston Belward, which, through being lost, was never put into force. He was not sure that it had value. If it had, all chance of the estate was gone for him; it would be his uncle's. Well, what did it matter? Yes, it did matter: Andree! For her? No, not for her. He would play straight. He would take his future as it came: he would not drop this paper into the water.

He smiled bitterly, got an envelope at a publichouse on the quay, wrote a few words in pencil on the document, and in a few moments it was on its way to Sir William Belward, who when he received it said:

"Worthless, quite worthless, but he has an honest mind—an honest mind!"

Meanwhile, Andree was in Paris. Leaving her bag at the Gare Montparnasse, she had gone straight to Ian Belward's house. She had lived years in the last few hours. She had had no sleep on the journey, and her mind had been strained unbearably. It had, however, a fixed idea, which shuttled in and out in a hundred shapes, but ever pointing to one end. She had determined on a painful thing—the only way.

She reached the house, and was admitted. In answer to questions, she had an appointment with monsieur. He was not within. Well, she would wait. She was motioned into the studio. She was outwardly calm. The servant presently recognised her. He had been to the menagerie, and he had seen her with Gaston. His manner changed instantly. Could he do anything? No, nothing. She was left alone. For a long time she sat motionless, then a sudden restlessness seized her. Her brain seemed a burning atmosphere, in which every thought, every thing showed with an unbearable intensity. The terrible clearness of it all—how it made her eyes, her heart ache! Her blood was beating hard against every pore. She felt that she would go mad if he did not come. Once she took out the stiletto she had concealed in the bosom of her cloak, and looked at it. She had always carried it when among the beasts at the menagerie, but had never yet used it.

Time passed. She felt ill; she became blind with pain. Presently the servant entered with a telegram. His master would not be back until the next morning.

Very well, she would return in the morning. She gave him money. He was not to say that she had called. In the Boulevard Montparnasse she took a cab. To the menagerie, she said to the driver. How strange it all looked: the Invalides, Notre Dame, the Tuileries Gardens, the Place de la Concorde! The innumerable lights were so near and yet so far: it was a kink of the brain, but she seemed withdrawn from them, not they from her. A woman passed with a baby in her arms. The light from a kiosk fell on it as she passed. What a pretty, sweet face it had. Why did it not have a pretty, delicate Breton cap? As she went on, that kept beating in her brain—why did not the child wear a dainty Breton cap—a white Breton cap? The face kept peeping from behind the lights—without the dainty Breton cap.

The menagerie at last. She dismissed the cab, went to a little door at the back of the building, and knocked. She was admitted. The care-taker exclaimed with pleasure. She wished to visit the animals? He would go with her; and he picked up a light. No, she would go alone. How were Hector and Balzac, and Antoinette? She took the keys. How cool and pleasant they were to the touch! The steel of the lantern too—how exquisitely soothing! He must lie down again: she would wake him as she came out. No, no, she would go alone.

She went to cage after cage. At last to that of the largest lions. There was a deep answering purr to her soft call. As she entered, she saw a heap moving in one corner—a lion lately bought. She spoke, and there was an angry growl. She wheeled to leave the cage, but her cloak caught the door, and it snapped shut.

Too late. A blow brought her to the ground. She had made no cry, and now she lay so still!

The watchman had fallen asleep again. In the early morning he remembered. The greyish golden dawn was creeping in, when he found her with two lions protecting, keeping guard over her, while another crouched snarling in a corner. There was no mark on her face.

The point of the stiletto which she had carried in her cloak had pierced her when she fell.

In a hotel near the Arc de Triomphe Alice Wingfield read the news. It was she who tenderly prepared the body for burial, who telegraphed to Gaston at Audierne, getting a reply from Jacques that he was not yet back from London. The next day Andree was found a quiet place in the cemetery at Montmartre.

In the evening Alice and her relative started for Audierne.

....

On board the Fleur d'Orange Gaston struggled with the problem. There was one thought ever coming. He shut it out at this point, and it crept in at that. He remembered when two men, old friends, discovered that one, unknowingly, had been living with the wife of the other. There was one too many—the situation was impossible. The men played a game of cards to see which should die. But they did not reckon with the other factor. It was the woman who died.

Was not his own situation far worse? With his uncle living—but no, no, it was out of the question! Yet Ian Belward had been shameless, a sensualist, who had wrecked the girl's happiness and his. He himself had done a mad thing in the eyes of the world, but it was more mad than wicked. Had this happened in the North with another man, how easily would the problem have been solved!

Go to his uncle and tell him that he must remove himself for ever from the situation? Demand it, force it? Impossible—this was Europe.

They arrived at Douarnenez. The diligence had gone. A fishing-boat was starting for Audierne. He decided to go by it. Breton fishermen are usually shy of storm to foolishness, and one or two of the crew urged the drunken skipper not to start, for there were signs of a south-west wind, too friendly to the Bay des Trepasses. The skipper was, however, cheerfully reckless, and growled down objection.

The boat came on with a sweet wind off the land for a time. Suddenly, when in the neighbourhood of Point du Raz, the wind drew ahead very squally, with rain in gusts out of the south-west. The skipper put the boat on the starboard tack, close-hauled and close-reefed the sails, keeping as near the wind as possible, with the hope of weathering the rocky point at the western extremity of the Bay des Trepasses. By that time there was a heavy sea running; night came on, and the weather grew very thick. They heard the breakers presently, but they could not make out the Point. Old sailor as he was, and knowing as well as any man the perilous ground, the skipper lost his drunken head this time, and presently lost his way also in the dark and murk of the storm.

At eight o'clock she struck. She was thrown on her side, a heavy sea broke over her, and they were all washed off. No one raised a cry. They were busy fighting Death.

Gaston was a strong swimmer. It did not occur to him that perhaps this was the easiest way out of the maze. He had ever been a fighter. The seas tossed him here and there. He saw faces about him for an instant— shaggy wild Breton faces—but they dropped away, he knew not where. The current kept driving him inshore. As in a dream, he could hear the breakers—the pumas on their tread-mill of death. How long would it last? How long before he would be beaten upon that tread-mill—fondled to death by those mad paws? Presently dreams came-kind, vague, distant dreams. His brain flew like a drunken dove to far points of the world and back again. A moment it rested. Andree! He had made no provision for her, none at all. He must live, he must fight on for her, the homeless girl, his wife.

He fought on and on. No longer in the water, as it seemed to him. He had travelled very far. He heard the clash of sabres, the distant roar of cannon, the beating of horses' hoofs—the thud-thud, tread-tread of an army. How reckless and wild it was! He stretched up his arm to strike- what was it? Something hard that bruised: then his whole body was dashed against the thing. He was back again, awake. With a last effort he drew himself up on a huge rock that stands lonely in the wash of the bay. Then he cried out, "Andree!" and fell senseless—safe.

The storm went down. The cold, fast-travelling moon came out, saw the one living thing in that wild bay, and hurried on into the dark again; but came and went so till morning, playing hide-and-seek with the man and his Ararat.

Daylight saw him, wet, haggard, broken, looking out over the waste of shaken water. Upon the shore glared the stone of the vanished City of Ys in the warm sun, and the fierce pumas trod their grumbling way. Sea- gulls flew about the quiet set figure, in whose brooding eyes there were at once despair and salvation.

He was standing between two worlds. He had had his great crisis, and his wounded soul rested for a moment ere he ventured out upon the highways again. He knew not how it was, but there had passed into him the dignity of sorrow and the joy of deliverance at the same time. He saw life's responsibilities clearer, duties swam grandly before him. It was a large dream, in which, for the time, he was not conscious of those troubles which, yesterday, had clenched his hands and knotted his forehead. He had come a step higher in the way of life, and into his spirit had flowed a new and sobered power. His heart was sore, but his mind was lifted up. The fatal wrangle of the pumas there below, the sound of it, would be in his ears for ever, but he had come above it; the searching vigour of the sun entered into his bones.

He knew that he was going back to England—to ample work and strong days, but he did not know that he was going alone. He did not know that Andree was gone forever; that she had found her true place: in his undying memory.

So intent was he, that at first he did not see a boat making into the bay towards him.

Milton Keynes UK
Ingram Content Group UK Ltd.
UKHW030743071024
449371UK00006B/595

9 789362 094483